4-6

D0944365

Csonka

Csonka

by Bill Gutman

A THISTLE BOOK

Published by

GROSSET & DUNLAP, INC.

New York

For Beth, with thanks

ACKNOWLEDGMENTS

The author wishes to thank the following people for their help in supplying background and photographic material for this book:

Joe Browne and Kay O'Reilly of the National Football League office; Mike Rathet of the Miami Dolphins; Larry Kimball, Sports Information Director at Syracuse University; Willis Walker of Stow High School; Sid Jacobson; and Bob and Sylvia Allen, whose fine photographs helped to complete this book.

PICTURE CREDITS: Bob and Sylvia Allen, pages ii, viii, 32, 37, 46–47, 48–49, 50, 60–61, 62, 64, 66, 68–69, 71, 75, 77, 79, 81, 84, 87; Miami Dolphins, pages 42–43, 55, 59; Wide World Photos, pages 7, 13, 28, 52, 57

CONTENTS

CHAPTER 1

Larry Csonka was born on a farm. He has always lived a rugged, outdoor life. He often got hurt, but he learned to take it at an early age. He grew tough and strong. The rugged life was good training for the future. Larry didn't know it then, but he was going to become the fullback of the world champion Miami Dolphins of the National Football League.

In each game Larry plays, he takes a bad beating. He runs very hard and fights for every inch he gains. So the defenders must hit him hard if they want to tackle him. He has to take the bumps. And he has to keep playing, even when he feels a lot of pain.

But his hard work has had its rewards. Most football fans agree that Larry Csonka is the best fullback in all of football. He gained more than 1,000 yards each season during the three seasons up to 1973. And even though he runs up the middle where there are more big tacklers, he still gains about five yards on every carry. Not many fullbacks can do that.

Being a fullback isn't an easy job. Larry pays a price for his toughness. After a game he has cuts and scratches all over his face and arms. It's hard for him to get to sleep, and he is very sore the next day. Most runners are sore after a game, but it's even worse for Larry because he runs and fights so hard.

Larry has been playing hard-fighting football for a long time. Before he joined the Dolphins he was a star fullback at Syracuse University. At Syracuse he broke the rushing records of players like Jim Brown, Ernie Davis, Jim Nance, and Floyd Little. All of them were very great football players. But Larry broke their records.

Before Larry played at Syracuse, he was the fullback on the Stow High School football team. That was in Stow, Ohio, where Larry was born on Christmas day in 1946. His parents, Joseph and Mildred Csonka, owned a 20-acre farm in Stow. That's where Larry grew up.

Larry's father was a hard-working man. Larry was one of six Csonka children. All the boys helped raise the crops and tend to the animals on the farm.

"It's a funny thing," Larry says today, "but I hated the farm until I was old enough to know better. I guess I hated it because my father made us work so hard. But that was good. Now when I think about it, I realize that it was a great life.

"It was great being outside all the time and having the animals around. There was a creek near our house and we had about 20 dogs on the farm. We also raised woodchucks and sometimes we found baby crows and raised them as pets. I'd really like to get a place like it someday so my kids could know what kind of life it is."

There were many good times on the farm, but Larry did get hurt sometimes. One day when he was six, he pulled his jacket from a wall above him. He forgot there was a brick holding it there. The brick fell, too, and broke Larry's nose.

Once, when he was feeding a cow,

4

the animal suddenly lifted its head. The cow's head hit Larry right in the face and broke his nose again. It got broken for a third time during a wrestling match in high school. Since then Larry has broken his nose another five or six times on the football field. So Larry's always known what it's like to get a good shot in the face.

When he was seven years old, Larry saw a football for the first time.

"I picked it up and looked at it," he remembers. "I didn't know what it was, but it was new and the leather really smelled good. It smelled so good I couldn't believe it."

Young Larry played baseball before he played football. He was on a Little League team and did very well. He was big, even then. He was so big, in fact, that the other, smaller kids didn't want him to play any more.

Maybe that's one reason he started

playing football. He played on a football team when he was still in grade school. He played hard even then, and he often came home covered with bruises. His father remembers one game when he really took a beating.

"Larry came home with a black eye and a puffed up mouth," said Mr. Csonka. "I saw the game and he really played his heart out. But the team lost and he was crying about it. I told him not to worry. He had played as well as he could and shouldn't feel sorry. I think that made him feel better."

Even though he sometimes got hurt, Larry loved the game right from the start. He kept playing. When he reached Stow High School he was big and strong, and a good football player. He had played all the positions as a youngster and liked fullback the best. And since he was so big and could run, the coach put him there.

arry likes kids. He was still at Syracuse when he
isited this hospital with his wife Pam (left).

"I wasn't real fast, but I could run hard and didn't get tired," says Larry. "I can thank the farm life for that. I was always running somewhere. Sometimes I was almost two miles from the house when my mom rang the dinner bell. I was always so hungry that I'd run all the way home without stopping. It was a long way to run."

Stow High School didn't have a very good team. They didn't play in a really good league, either. Most of the schools were small and there weren't many good players. But Larry already weighed more than 200 pounds and he was almost impossible to tackle. By the time he was a senior, there were scouts from many colleges coming to see him play.

At Stow High School, Larry saw how sports can suddenly make a hero out of a person. Some of his classmates weren't nice to him at first. But when they saw he was really a good football player they became friendly. He didn't like that.

"I don't think people should act that way," he said. "The same kids who wouldn't look at me before they knew I played football were the first ones around when I became one of the better players on the team. But they certainly didn't like me for *me*. They didn't like Larry Csonka, person. They liked Larry Csonka, football star.

"As for football, it was fun all the way. I loved it from the first day I went out for the team. I remember saying then, 'Oh, man, this is the game for me.'" He was right about that!

CHAPTER 2

Larry was a star at Stow High for three years. He had some great games. People from Stow will never forget his hard running. Then it was time for him to think about college. Almost 40 schools sent scouts to see him play. And almost all of them wanted him.

He was a very strong fullback in high school. He was still growing, and although he didn't run very fast, he never lost the ball. He was also a fine blocker. And he played when he was hurt. In other words, he was a winner.

Scouts and coaches like that. They call it a good football attitude. And a good attitude is very important to an athlete.

Larry looked very carefully at the schools that wanted him. Many of the scouts told him he was getting too big to be a fullback. They said he might weigh 250 or 260 pounds some day. They said he should be a linebacker or maybe a guard. But Larry wanted to be a fullback. He wanted to carry the football.

Because of this he said no to many of the schools. He decided to pick between Clemson in South Carolina and Syracuse in upstate New York. Finally he made the choice. He would go to Syracuse and play with the Orangemen. (That is the nickname of the Syracuse team.)

"It wasn't easy making up my mind," said Larry. "But I looked at the two schools and thought Syracuse would be best for me. First of all, they said I'd get a good chance at playing fullback. They said I might be a linebacker, too, but at least I'd get a chance. And the school wasn't big. I didn't want a real big school. But they played many top teams in football, so I'd be playing against the best.

"There was something else, too. I knew that Syracuse loved to run the football. They always had good runners there and if I got a chance to play fullback I'd get plenty of chances to run with the ball."

That was true, all right. The Orangemen love to run the ball. Jim Brown was the first all-American runner there in the mid-1950's. He went on to become one of the greatest pro runners ever. Ernie Davis came next, then big Jim Nance, then speedy Floyd Little. They were all great, record-breaking runners.

12   Young Larry was a bruising fullback for Syracuse University.

Larry went to Syracuse in the fall of 1964. He weighed almost 230 pounds and stood nearly 6 feet 3 inches tall. And he was still growing. He played on the freshman team that year. He played fullback and linebacker. And he was very good at both positions.

The regular team had a good year. They won seven and lost just three. The star of the team was halfback Floyd Little. He was a year ahead of Larry. During the 1964 season he gained 828 yards. Syracuse coach Ben Schwartzwalder thought Little would take care of the running game in 1965, too. So he decided to make Larry Csonka a linebacker.

Larry didn't like the move, but he said he'd try it. For the first three games that year he was a linebacker. And he was a good one. He was a hard tackler and it wasn't easy to block him out of the play. He was very strong.

The team won its first two games. Then it lost to the University of Miami, 24–0.

In that game the Miami defense was waiting for Floyd Little. They knew he was going to get the ball and they followed him wherever he went. Little didn't have a chance. Coach Schwartzwalder knew that other teams would start doing the same thing. He needed a better fullback to help Little. He decided to give Larry Csonka the first try.

"I remember when Larry decided to come to Syracuse," said the coach. "His father told me I was getting the best fullback I ever had. Well, I decided it was time to give Larry a chance. It turned out to be the smartest thing I've done in 23 years of coaching."

When they made Larry a fullback they expected him to block for Floyd

Little. If he did that well, it would be enough. Little was so good that he could carry the running load. But it didn't take the team long to find out that when Larry got the ball, he was a very hard man to stop.

He ran like a truck. When he was hit by someone he just shifted into high gear and kept going. It always took more than one man to bring him down. Sometimes four or five had to do it. He would just drag the tacklers along on his broad back. Suddenly Syracuse had the best running attack in the whole country.

"Larry had this little trick," said an old friend of his. "Just before he was hit, he would drop his head and ram it into the tackler. He was so strong that he would always plow along for another three yards or so before he was stopped."

At that time, Floyd Little was still the star. Most of the stories were about him. He was truly a great runner. But Larry was getting better with each passing week.

In the final game of the year, Syracuse played West Virginia University. Larry was running very well that day. Every time he carried the ball he made good yardage. And they kept giving him the ball. He was running so hard that the West Virginia tacklers didn't seem to want to get in his way.

When the game was over, Syracuse had its seventh win of the year (against three losses), 41–19. And Larry had gained 216 yards. That was a new school record. Not Brown, Davis, Nance, or Little had ever gained so much in a single game. Larry was very happy. He had wanted a chance to play fullback. And when he got it, he had done better than anyone thought possible.

Nineteen sixty-five was also a great year for Floyd Little, who gained 1,065 yards on 193 carries and was an all-American. But Larry wasn't far behind. In just seven games he gained 795 yards on 136 carries. Not bad for a sophomore fullback who had two more years to play.

Syracuse had a really good team in 1966. Little was still an exciting runner. And Larry was even better than before. The team lost its first two games, but after that they were unbeatable. The Orangemen won eight straight games and were one of the ten best teams in the country. And as the season went on, Larry began to get the ball more and more. Even more than Floyd Little.

Defenders playing against Syracuse still expected Floyd Little to do most of the running. They would set up the defense to stop his lightning-quick sweeps around the end.

Knowing this, the Syracuse quarterback would often fake a sweep to Floyd and give the ball to Larry instead. Then Larry would blast right up the middle. By the time the surprised defense stopped him, Csonka had another big gain. By the end of the year they knew he was coming, but they still couldn't stop him.

That year (1966) Larry Csonka was the top runner on the Syracuse team. Floyd Little gained 811 yards, carrying the ball 162 times, but Larry carried 197 times and gained 1,012 yards. Both Larry and Floyd were all-America now.

Floyd Little graduated the next

June. He finished his Syracuse career with 2,704 yards on 504 carries. Both totals were new school records. Floyd went on to become an all-pro with the NFL Denver Broncos. Larry had another year left. Now he'd be the only star in the backfield.

CHAPTER 3

With Floyd Little gone, Larry knew he might have a problem. For the past two seasons, Floyd had run beside Larry. The defenses had to worry about both, Floyd outside and Larry inside. Now only Larry was there. Defenders knew he'd be coming straight at them. There was no one to run outside. Many people thought Larry wouldn't have a good year because of this.

But they just couldn't stop Larry Csonka. He weighed 240 pounds and was strong as a bull. He carried and carried, and ran over anyone who was in the way. On one play early in the season he dragged four tacklers some 14 yards before going down. The whole country began to look toward Syracuse to see what this one-man army was like.

The team won its first two games with Larry as the big star. Then against Maryland he set another record by carrying the ball 43 times, leading the team to a 7–3 win. Near the end of the game Syracuse wanted to keep the ball and use up time on the block. The Orange quarterback gave the ball to Larry eight straight times. Each time he just ran straight at the Maryland defenders. But they fell from his path like bowling pins. He gained 46 yards on those eight carries. He made three first downs and ate up minutes of valuable time.

Navy upset Syracuse the next week.

But Larry played so well that Navy coach Bill Elias said:

"Csonka is good enough to play for any National Football League team, and he's good enough to do it right now!"

The next week Larry gained 202 yards against California. Then came the big game with Penn State. Both Penn State and Syracuse wanted to be the best team in the East. Joe Paterno, the coach of Penn State, was worried about one thing — stopping Larry Csonka.

"He's got to be the greatest fullback in the country," said Paterno. "If you don't get a two-score lead on them he controls the game, and there's no way you can stop him."

Penn State did get a big lead that afternoon, but Larry gained 115 yards and gave Penn State a lot to worry about before they finally won, 29–20.

"We won, but we didn't stop Csonka," said Joe Paterno. "The man is simply a great, great fullback."

That 1967 season wasn't easy for Larry. He was taking a real beating. After the Pittsburgh game the next week, Larry held out his hands for reporters. Both were battered and swollen. Doctors discovered a broken bone in one of them. But he didn't miss a game. His hands were in such bad shape that his father had to take his pads off. Larry had no feeling in his fingers.

"They've really been giving it to me inside this year," he said. "They couldn't do it last year because I had Floyd Little with me then. Now they know what's coming and they're ready."

Coach Schwartzwalder also knew

about the punishment his star fullback was taking.

"The man takes an awful beating every week, no matter what team we play. But never once has he complained about it or asked for any special favors, either in practice or a game."

Now Larry's college career was coming to an end. There were only a couple of games left. The eighth game that year was against Holy Cross. Larry was having a good day. He made a big gain early in the game when suddenly everything stopped. There was an announcement on the P.A. system.

LADIES AND GENTLEMEN. LARRY CSONKA HAS JUST BROKEN FLOYD LITTLE'S ALL-TIME SYRACUSE RUSHING RECORD!

So there it was. Larry was the new rushing king at Syracuse. He had gained more yards than all those great runners before him. It was a feat to be proud of.

Larry closed his Syracuse career by leading his team to a 32–14 upset of UCLA. The Orangemen were 8–2 again with Larry once more an all-American.

In 1967, Larry had carried the ball 261 times. That was a new record. He gained 1,127 yards for another record. His three-year totals were 2,934 yards on 594 carries. He also had 14 100-yard games. His rushing average had dropped from 5.1 his junior year to 4.3 as a senior. But that was because there was no Floyd Little around to take the pressure off. Coach Schwartzwalder knew what a winner Larry was.

"Larry has got to be the most valuable player I've ever coached," he said. "This year is a perfect example. He did more with less blocking than any other runner we've had. Every team we played knew he was coming at them and they beat him up all year. But he just kept rolling, getting so many of those yards on his own. It's amazing that he could average 4.3 yards a crack under those conditions."

Larry was sad to leave Syracuse. He really liked it there. But it was time to move on and there was just one thing he wanted to do. He wanted to play professional football. He didn't know where he would play, but he knew he'd be ready.

Meanwhile, he decided to play in as many extra games as he could. In December there was the East-West Shrine Game in San Francisco. Larry started at fullback for the East and played very well. Then, in January of 1968, he got the news. He was the number one draft choice of the Miami Dolphins.

The Dolphins were a new team.

After a record-breaking college career, Larry signed his first contract with the Miami Dolphins of the NFL. Miami's Joe Robbie looks very happy to have Larry with the team.

They had started to play in 1966 and they weren't very good. But they were trying to build with talented, young players. Larry liked that. He began discussions about the contract.

He wanted to show the Dolphins what he could do. That spring he played in the Hula Bowl game in Hawaii and ran so well he was named the Outstanding Back of the game. He weighed 250 pounds and the Dolphins liked what they saw.

Larry asked for a lot of money——over $200,000. But the Dolphins thought it was too much. They wouldn't pay what he asked. For a while, Larry thought about playing in Canada, in the Canadian League. That was because he loved the outdoors and knew he'd love living in Canada. He was afraid that Miami would be like so many big cities, very crowded and dirty.

But when he visited Miami he was surprised. There weren't many big factories, smog, or smoke. Finally, he agreed to a contract with the Dolphins. He signed to play for about $100,000, spread over several seasons.

Then it was back to football. The Dolphins' training camp would begin in mid-July. Before that, Larry played in the Coaches All-America game in Atlanta and was once again the star. He carried 28 times for 88 yards and was named the game's Most Valuable Player, even though his team lost. He showed the pros he could carry a big work load. From there he went to Chicago to play in the College All-Star Game. This time the college stars would be meeting the champion Green Bay Packers.

This is never an easy game for the college stars. The pro champs are always ready. They don't want to lose to a group of collegians. And the All-Stars don't have much time to practice as a team.

It's usually the Stars' defense that crumbles first, and that's what happened in the 1968 game. Packer quarterback Bart Starr picked apart the All-Star defense. He hit his good receivers with ease. By the half it was 24–3 in favor of Green Bay.

The Packers had the ball so much in the first half that Larry didn't get a real chance. But in the second half he started rolling.

In the end, the Packers won 34–17, but Larry Csonka was once again the best college·player on the field. He had run through the great Packer defense. He had carried the ball 18 times and gained 95 yards. That was better than both Packer backs, Donny Anderson and Jim Grabowski, to-

gether. Larry was named the Most Valuable Player once more. All-Star coach Norm Van Brocklin couldn't say enough about him.

"Larry is a real strong-man," said Van Brocklin. "And he has a great attitude. He can find the openings, and he has the sense to know when to turn on the speed. I don't think there's any question about his power. Ask the Packers who tried to stop him."

As for Larry, he was really excited. "Playing against the Packers was like a dream come true for me. Every time I'd run by one of their linebackers I'd feel as if I passed a test. They're so great." Now the time had come to join the pros.

Larry works out before the season starts. You can see how strong his legs are. That's one reason he's so hard to tackle.

CHAPTER 4

When he finally got to the Dolphins' camp Larry learned he was only the number two fullback. A man named Stan Mitchell was number one because he had played the position the year before. Larry would have to beat him out.

In his second exhibition game Larry gained 90 yards on 22 carries. It looked good, but he wasn't happy.

"I played a stupid game," he said. "I'm trying to get everything on my own. I've got to learn to follow my blockers. That's very important in pro ball. I'm just not going through the holes they make for me."

Miami quarterback Bob Griese said the same thing. "Larry kept missing the holes. If he weren't so big and strong he would have been stopped. He still has a lot to learn."

Pro football is a lot harder than college ball. The players are bigger and faster. They all want to win. Sometimes players who are very good in college don't do as well in the pros. Sometimes it takes a few years to get a starting position. But Larry happened to get a chance right away. Stan Mitchell hurt his knee and Larry became number one.

There were now two rookies in the Miami backfield — Larry and the halfback, Jim Kiick, a 215-pounder from Wyoming. Kiick wasn't really fast, but he followed his blockers well. He was also an excellent pass receiver.

He and Larry became friends very quickly. Soon they would be riding high as a backfield combination.

Larry's first game was against the Houston Oilers. He was nervous at the beginning. He didn't do very well, gaining just 26 yards. But he didn't make any mistakes, either. However, the defense did make mistakes and the team lost, 24–10.

Two more losses followed. Then Csonka and Kiick had their first really big day. It was against the Oilers again, and this time quarterback Griese stayed with the running game. Kiick and Csonka battered away at the Houston line. When the game ended, Miami had a 24–7 win. Kiick had run for 104 yards and Larry for 82. People were beginning to say that Miami had the best young backfield in the league.

36 This was a familiar scene during Larry's first two years with the Dolphins. He didn't break his falls with his arm then, and he often hurt his head.

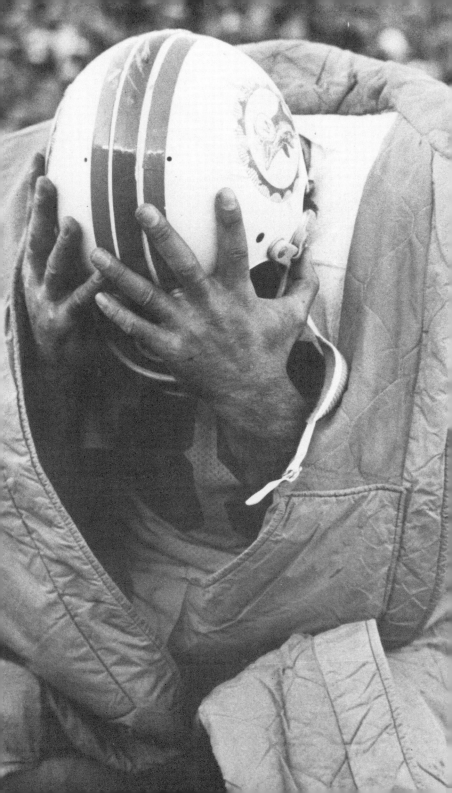

The next week Larry got his first serious injury. Ever since the days at Syracuse, he had been running head first. He lowered his head and rammed into tacklers, hoping to get a few more yards. Some coaches told him it was risky. They said he would hurt his head sooner or later. But Larry liked to run that way. It was a habit. Even when he didn't want to, he found himself running head first.

He did it again in the game at Buffalo in the fourth quarter. After the pile-up, Larry was still lying on the field. He was knocked out.

The doctor woke him up. They brought out a stretcher to carry him off the field. Larry wouldn't allow it.

"No way," he growled. "I walked in here and I'm walking out. You're not going to carry me out in front of all these people."

So Larry made it to the sidelines.

Then he blacked out again. At the hospital they said he had a concussion. He'd miss at least one game.

"I don't know how it happened," he said, later. "Maybe a helmet got me or I was kicked. I remember lying on the ground behind the bench and feeling some guy stepping on my hand. It was a photographer trying to get a picture of me half-dead!"

Larry was lucky. He made a fast recovery and two weeks later he had a good game against Cincinnati. He gained 97 yards, including one run of 40 yards. Then he got another head injury. The doctors were beginning to worry about him. Head injuries are very serious. They gave him a special helmet to wear. It had a lot of extra padding.

In spite of his injuries, it wasn't a bad rookie year for Larry. He had gained 540 yards on 138 carries for a

3.9 average. Kiick had 621 yards and a 3.8 average. The team was better, too. The Dolphins finished at 5–8–1, their best record yet.

When the 1969 season began, Larry's coach, George Wilson, tried to teach him to carry the ball with one arm. That way, he could use the other arm to protect his head and break his falls. But Larry still carried with both arms. His head hit his opponents before any other part of his body. And it hit the ground first, too.

Sure enough, he hurt his head again as soon as the pre-season games started. He began getting bad headaches. An examination showed a cracked bone in the side of his head. He'd miss about a month. But the doctors told him if he kept hurting his head he might have to quit. This really upset Larry. He loved the game so much.

"I don't care about the pain in my

head," he said. "The real pain is waiting to see if some doctor is going to tell me to quit."

Larry missed the first three games of the season. Then he came back when Stan Mitchell was hurt again. He played well. He started using his arm to break his falls, and he was leading with his shoulders instead of his head. The injury seemed to have healed. He wasn't getting headaches any more.

In the eighth game that year the Dolphins played the Boston Patriots. Larry was really good that day. He gained 121 yards on 16 carries. He also ran 54 yards for a touchdown. It was his best game as a pro and he really felt good about it.

"Right now I have no injuries," he said. "I hope it stays that way. The head thing seems to be all gone and I'm glad about that."

Larry finished the season with 566

Larry has learned to use his arm to break his fall. He doesn't want any more head injuries.

yards on 131 carries. He had a 4.3 average, and that was good. He had also caught 21 passes for 183 yards. Once the head injury healed, he had a good year.

But the Dolphins had not had a good year. The team dropped to a 3–10–1 record and Coach Wilson was fired. He was replaced by Don Shula, who had been a winning coach with the Baltimore Colts.

Shula quickly began getting new players. He made trades and signed some free agents. He was in a hurry for the Dolphins to start winning. He worked hard to give the team a better defense. He also made a trade for Paul Warfield, one of the best pass receivers in the league.

Shula didn't touch the backfield. Quarterback Griese, halfback Kiick, and fullback Csonka would remain.

The only new backfield player was speedy halfback Mercury Morris, who was a good outside runner.

Coach Shula loved having a fullback like Larry. But he didn't want him to be too heavy. He asked Larry to get his weight down to 235. Then he'd be even faster, but just as strong.

"Larry didn't argue when we asked him to lose weight," said an assistant coach. "He just did it. But he's that kind of player. He does everything you want without complaint. And he always gives everything he has out on the field. He's a bruising type of fullback who can break tackles and gain four or five yards up the middle without much trouble."

The Dolphins were a different team in 1970. Shula made them winners overnight. The defense was much better and the offense was, too. For the

Blocking is very important for a fullback. Here Larry works on his pass-protection blocking for the quarterback.

Dolphin against Dolphin. It's hard to believe teammates hit each other so hard in practice. But it's the
only way to get ready for the real game.

Against the Green Bay Packers, Larry goes over the middle for a first down.

first time Larry didn't have a single injury. He was the team's best runner all year long.

Larry ran for 874 yards on 193 carries. He had two 100-yard games and was on the verge of being a real star. Kiick had more than 650 yards and Morris more than 400. The Dolphin running game was really working.

The Miami record jumped to 10–4. The team didn't win its division, but still made it into the playoffs. There, the Dolphins lost to powerful Oakland, 21–14. But it looked as if the team was becoming very good.

CHAPTER 5

By now, Larry Csonka and Jim Kiick were real pals, both on and off the field. People always thought of them together. They had new nicknames. They became known as "Butch Cassidy and the Sundance Kid" after the characters in the popular movie about old-time western outlaws. Kiick was Butch and Larry was Sundance. The nicknames were fun for Larry and Jim. The two stars even dressed in old western clothes and let photographers take pictures of them.

On the field they helped each other.

Larry (left) and Jim Kiick pose for the cameras in their Butch Cassidy and Sundance Kid outfits. The two runners are very good friends off and on the field.

When one carried the ball, the other blocked for him. And both performed well.

"We know each other's moves very well," said Larry. "When I'm running I know just how Jim will take the man out and I go the other way. And he knows what I like to do and tries to block the best way. When he's running the same thing works. He knows how I block and I know how he likes to run."

"Butch" and "Sundance" made news again before the 1971 season. They held out for more money. And they even did that together. Coach Shula didn't like it and he fined them for missing training camp. Finally the two backs signed. They got more money, though not as much as they had asked for. Then they paid their fine. Larry, Jim, and the coach all agreed that the fine would go to a bad-

Larry and Jim during a game. They're a couple of pretty tough customers.

ly injured high school player. That was a very good cause.

Larry still loved football, but he wanted to be well paid for it. He knew he couldn't play forever. So he had to think about the future. Larry had married while he was still at Syracuse. Now he had two boys, Doug and Paul. His wife, Pam, and the children were very important to him. He wanted to have enough to support them when he couldn't play any more.

The 1971 season was a great one for Larry, Jim, and the Dolphins. The team won the AFC Eastern Division title with a 10–3–1 record. Larry had some big days, including a 137-yard game against the Jets. He finished with 1,051 yards on 195 carries. Gaining over 1,000 yards meant a lot to Larry, and his 5.4 average was among the best in the league.

56   When *Esquire Magazine* did a story on Larry and Jim they dressed them up like a couple of "dudes."

Not many fullbacks get five yards on every carry. But Larry was now running outside sweeps as well as the tough stuff up the middle. He had a great guard, Larry Little, who blocked for him on sweeps.

"When I go out on a sweep behind Little I can see fear in the eyes of the cornerbacks," he said. "They know how hard he is going to hit them. Sometimes I just grab the back of his shirt and let him pull me through. It's really great to have a guy like that blocking for you."

In the first game of the playoffs that year the Dolphins played a very good team, the Kansas City Chiefs. It was a real battle. First the Dolphins led. Then the Chiefs led. With just minutes left, quarterback Griese passed to tight end Marv Fleming for a TD. The Dolphins had tied the game. The gun sounded. Now the game

The pro game is rough. In this game against the Jets, Larry's favorite blocker, Larry Little (66), has been knocked down and Zonk has to get the yards on his own.

This is more like it. Tackle Norm Evans (73) blocks
his man, while guard Larry Little (66) swings out in
front of Zonk. The Dolphins gained a lot of yards on
this play.

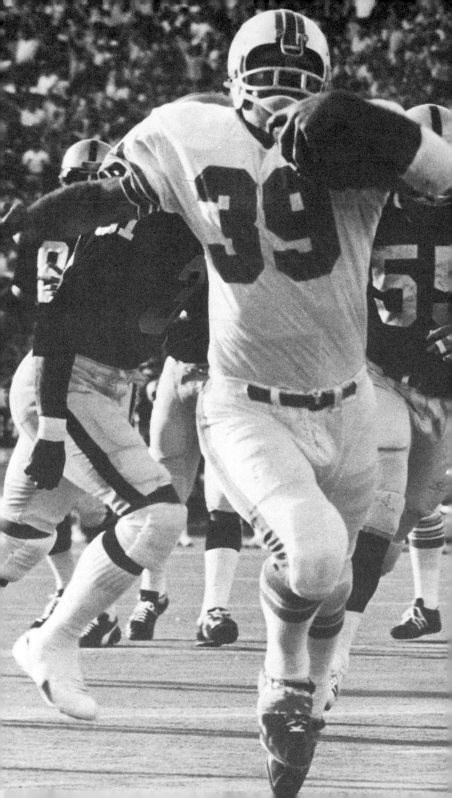

was in "sudden death" overtime. That meant the first team to score any points would win.

Sudden death games are very exciting. They only happen in the playoffs. Each team missed a field goal in the first overtime. The game went into a second overtime period. It was now the longest game in football history.

All the players were really tired. They weren't used to playing almost six periods of football. Something had to give. Finally the Dolphins started moving. The Kansas City defense didn't expect the tired runners to do much. They were waiting for the pass.

Then Larry took off on a sweep. He turned the corner, and cut back inside. It was hard to believe he could still run so hard. When two Chief defenders caught him, he dragged them another five yards until they got help.

At first they said that Larry was too slow. Wrong! Here, the big guy is running away from the defenders. A slow back couldn't average five yards a carry the way Larry does.

He had run for 29 yards and brought the Dolphins into K.C. territory.

Several plays later Griese passed to Paul Warfield, bringing the ball to the 30. Then Garo Yepremian came on and kicked a 37-yard field goal. Miami had won the game, 27–24.

The Dolphins won the AFC championship the next week, beating Baltimore, 21–0. They were going to the Super Bowl. Then the team finally had a bad game. Dallas whipped the Dolphins, 24–3, for the world championship. But Miami had come a long way. Many people thought the Dolphins would soon be football's next superteam.

Larry never lets up. He even blocks on extra-point tries. Holder Carl Noonan (on one knee) is ready for the snap, and a tired Larry is ready to make his block.

Larry became more famous with each year. Here he talks with sportscaster Howard Cosell at the Dolphins' training camp.

CHAPTER 6

Larry was a hero now. He was an all-pro. Everyone wanted to talk to the Sundance Kid. But Larry felt it was very important, especially for youngsters, to look at football players as real people.

"Football and football players should not be looked at as so special," he said. "I love the game. I could never find as much enjoyment in other things. But we shouldn't make our kids feel that football is so important."

This is a new twist. Halfback Kiick (21) and fullback
Cosell (7). That must make Larry the coach! This was
part of a television show that Howard Cosell did on
the Dolphins.

"One day I was asked to come and watch a team of 10- and 11-year-old kids work out. As soon as I got there the coach began putting them through drills. Suddenly, he began running a 'nutcracker' drill, one of the roughest ones the pros use. Here he was, doing it with these little kids.

"Well, sure enough, one little guy gets hurt, real bad. So what does the coach do? He starts screaming at the kid to stop crying and act like a man. He forced the kid to get up and continue. Later we found the kid's nose was broken.

"My point is that parents should be very careful about the kind of man they trust their kids with. A coach like the one I saw can really hurt a youngster. Besides, there's no need to rush a kid into tackle. Let him play flag or touch football for a while. Let him have fun. There's plenty of time for tackle later."

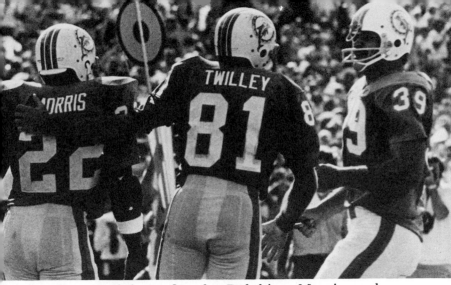

Another touchdown for the Dolphins. Morris, end Howard Twilley, and Larry congratulate each other after the score. Fans have seen this many times during the past few seasons.

In 1972 the Dolphins didn't lose a single game. Three reasons were halfback Mercury Morris (22), Larry, and quarterback Bob Griese (12).

The 1972 season is one Larry and his Dolphin teammates will never forget. The team was getting better and better. The defense was one of the best in the league. And the offense was hard to stop. Larry just powered behind his fine blockers for big gains. Mercury Morris was playing more and he was proving to be a great runner. He ran to the outside very well. Kiick was still steady and sure.

Miami won its first four games with little trouble. Then, in the fifth game, quarterback Griese broke his ankle. Now many people thought the Dolphins would lose. But veteran Earl Morrall took over and the team kept winning.

Every week someone said the Dolphins would lose. And every week they still won. The impossible was happening. No NFL team had ever won all of its 14 games. But the Dolphins were doing it. They finished by beating St. Louis, New England, the Giants, and Baltimore for a perfect, 14–0–0 record!

Larry was great again. He gained 1,117 yards on 213 carries for a 5.2 average. He was second to O. J. Simpson in AFC rushing. Morris finished with 1,000 yards even. Kiick had more than 500. Together, they set a new NFL rushing record (later broken by the Buffalo Bills). Now the playoffs were coming. The team really wanted to win the Super Bowl.

There were still some people who didn't believe the Dolphins were that good. They said Miami had played against teams that were easy to beat. The playoffs would be the real challenge.

The first game was a close one against the Cleveland Browns. But Miami scored in the final minutes to win, 20–14. Then came tough Pittsburgh. The Steelers led early, but Miami came on to win it, 21–17. In that game, Bob Griese came back. His broken ankle had healed. He would be the starter in the Super Bowl game against the Washington Redskins.

Now the Dolphins really showed their stuff. Griese hit his first six passes in a row. One was a TD pass to end Howard Twilley in the first period. Then Kiick scored in the second period. It was 14–0. That was all the scoring for Miami, but it was enough.

In the second half the Dolphins controlled the game. Larry began to eat up the yards. He had a 49-yard run late in the game and finished with 112 yards on just 15 carries. Washington scored late, but when the game ended, the Dolphins had won, 14–7.

74   Football used to be a cold-weather game. But it's always hot in Miami. Larry uses a towel to escape the
hot sun on the bench.

The team had done it. They'd won 17 straight games. They were champions of the world.

"This is something we all worked hard for," said Larry. "In 1970, we were happy just to make the playoffs. Last year getting to the Super Bowl was the big thing. This year we knew we had to win it. Next year we've got to win it again."

In 1973, the Dolphins kept getting better and better. The team had young players almost at all the positions. The defense was the best in the league. The offense was very powerful.

The team finished with a 12–2 record and then rolled into the playoffs. Larry had another 1,000-yard season and Mercury Morris missed by just a few yards. Late in the season the Dolphins seemed really unbeatable. As soon as they got the ball they'd just

Sometimes football looks neat, clean, and easy . . .

drive down for a TD. No team was able to stop them.

In the 1973 playoffs the Dolphins really proved, once and for all, that they were football's best team. In the first round Miami played the Cincinnati Bengals. The Dolphins took the opening kickoff and marched in for a score. Then they scored again. Then again. It was 21–0 before the Bengals could get a point. It ended at 34–16. Morris gained 106 yards in that one and Larry ran for 71.

Oakland came next. The Raiders were big and tough as usual. But they didn't bother Miami. Once again the Dolphins got the ball and marched right in for a score. Then the ground game took over. Larry was great. He ran past the surprised Raiders as if they were lightweights. Time and again he got the call and ripped off big gains.

. . . Other times it's dirty, rough, and hard. Here, it looks like another broken nose for Larry.

When Larry wasn't running inside, Mercury or Kiick were running outside. at the end, Larry had 117 yards. And the Dolphins won, 27–10. They'd be going to the Super Bowl once more.

Larry had carried the football 29 times in the Oakland game. The team record was 26. He was tired after the game, but very happy.

"Sure, I'm tired," he said. "But I'm not as tired as I used to be when I wasn't going anywhere. If you have the blocking and they give you daylight, you run for yardage. When I have a good day it's because my offensive line is doing the job. They usually do."

In the Super Bowl game the Dolphins would play the Minnesota Vikings. The Vikings were also a strong team. Fran Tarkenton was the quarterback and the defense was one of the best. It would be a real test.

Sometimes the fans don't see everything. On the sidelines Larry holds his nose after getting another shot. Back on the field, he'll act as if nothing had happened. That's football.

Miami got the ball at the start. Right away quarterback Griese began giving the pigskin to Larry. The big fullback just took it straight at the Viking defense. He was like a steamroller, leaving the Vikings behind in a cloud of dust.

Once again Miami marched downfield. Larry scored from the five and the Dolphins had the lead, 7–0. Minnesota couldn't move and Miami got the ball back. Once again they started rolling. This time Kiick scored and it was 14–0. A Yepremian field goal made it 17–0 in the second period. Larry ran for another TD in the third to make it 24–0.

For the rest of the game Larry just kept running over the Vikings. His line was great. Men like Norm Evans, Larry Little, Jim Langer, and Bob Kuechenberg were punishing the Vikings. Larry did his share, too. The hitting was very hard.

In the second half it was almost Larry Csonka against the Vikings. He was controlling the game the way he used to at Syracuse. His running kept the Viking defense on the field. That meant Tarkenton and the offense never really had a chance to get started. When the game ended, the Dolphins had won their second straight Super Bowl, 24–7. Only the Green Bay Packers had done that before.

As for Larry, he set records once again. He had carried the ball an amazing 33 times and gained 145 yards — two Super Bowl records. He was also named the game's Most Valuable Player. Miami was the best team in football and Larry was the best fullback in the game.

It looked as if Larry had a long career ahead of him in Miami. But in March of 1974, there was a surprise announcement. Larry, Jim Kiick, and

Paul Warfield announced that they were going to play in a new league. It was called the World Football League (WFL). The three Miami players would get a great deal of money for "jumping" to a team in the WFL.

"I don't like leaving the Dolphins," Larry said. "But I have to think about my family. This will make it a lot easier when I retire."

The rules say that the three players must stay with Miami for the 1974 season. Then they are free to go to their new team. Other star NFL players (such as Calvin Hill, Ken Stabler and Ted Kwalick) have jumped to the WFL. Whenever a new league is formed, the star players from the old league can get a lot of money to switch.

Miami fans cannot really be angry with Larry. It would be hard for anyone to turn down a million dollars.

Larry clowns with assistant trainer Stan Taylor. Taylor probably bandaged Larry's leg.

That's what Larry will be getting with his new team. He has played great football for the Dolphins. In fact, he has played great football wherever he's been. And he will keep playing great football no matter what team he is playing for.

That's because Larry Csonka loves the game. He's one of the toughest and best there is. It would be hard to find a better fullback anywhere.

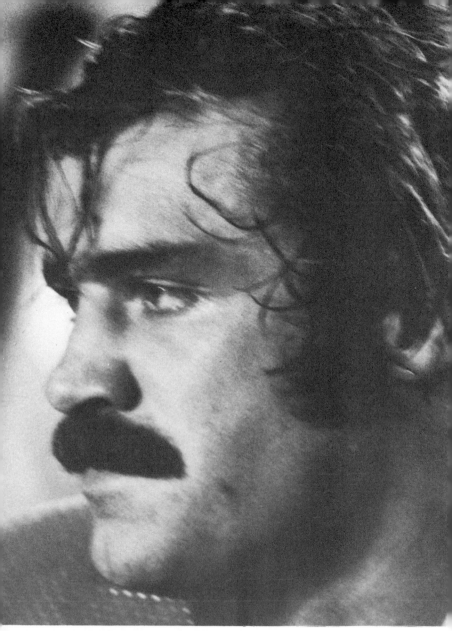

It's a quiet serious moment for Larry. Maybe he's thinking about, his future in the World Football League.

LARRY CSONKA'S RECORD

College Statistics

Year	Att.	Yds.	Aver.
1965	136	795	5.8
1966	197	1,012	5.1
1967	261	1,127	4.3
Totals	594	2,934	4.9

Pro Statistics

Year	Att.	Yds.	Aver.	Longest Gain	TD's
1968	138	540	3.9	40	6
1969	131	566	4.3	54	2
1970	193	874	4.5	53	6
1971	195	1,051	5.4	28	7
1972	213	1,117	5.2	45	6
1973	219	1,003	4.6	25	5
Totals	1,089	5,151	4.7	54	32

All-Time Syracuse Rushers

Name	Att.	Yds.
1. **Larry Csonka**	**594**	**2,934**
2. Floyd Little	504	2,704
3. Ernie Davis	360	2,386
4. Jim Brown	361	2,091
5. Jim Nance	325	1,605